JOAN
CHITTISTER

The ART of LIFE

Monastic wisdom for every day

For more information
about Joan Chittister, osb,
please visit her website
www.joanchittister.org

Twenty-Third Publications
A Division of Bayard
One Montauk Avenue, Suite 200
New London, CT 06320
(860) 437-3012 or (800) 321-0411
www.23rdpublications.com

ART CREDITS *January:* © ARTOTHEK ▪ *February:* © U. Edelmann - Städel Museum - ARTOTHEK
▪ *March:* © ARTOTHEK ▪ *April:* © Christie's Images Ltd - ARTOTHEK ▪ *May:* © Peter Willi
- ARTOTHEK ▪ *June:* © ARTOTHEK ▪ *July:* © Peter Willi - ARTOTHEK ▪ *August:* © Jochen
Remmer - ARTOTHEK ▪ *September:* © Peter Willi - ARTOTHEK ▪ *October:* © ALINARI -
ARTOTHEK ▪ *November:* © ARTOTHEK ▪ *December:* © ARTOTHEK

ISBN 978-1-58595-891-7
Library of Congress Control Number: 2012918695

Printed in the U.S.A.

CONTENTS

6
January
To Go
Light-
Footed
Through
Life

16
February
The Age of
Innocence

25
March
"Give Us
Bread and
Roses"

36
April
The
Solitude
of Night

45
May
Of
Dreams
and
Memories

55
June
Look!
One White
Iris

65
July
On Your
Mark, Get
Set, Play

74
August
Our
Unplayed
Melodies

82
September
The Gift
of Work

93
October
Love to
Wonder

104
November
To Look
at a Thing

114
December
O Come Let
Us Adore...

THE ART OF LIFE

JANUARY

DEER IN THE SNOW » (REHEIM SCHNEE 1911) » PUBLIC DOMAIN » BY FRANZ MARC

TO GO LIGHT-FOOTED
THROUGH LIFE

There is a deer in me—*made for running, for scampering while the rest of the world around me walks. I am made to find and drink from foreign streams. I am meant to go light-footed through life. So what am I doing in "stability" and "community," in a lifetime of "Rules" and hierarchy and patriarchy masking as "a woman's lifestyle"?*

But then, on the other hand, how can anyone move freely unless they are rooted in a worldview that is stable and a community that is empowering and a discipline that is strengthening? Disciplined, meaning stretched beyond ourselves to the best of ourselves. Like the well-trained Olympian, like the well-schooled scholar, like the well-formed soul.

It's easy to bounce through life—going here, trying that, tasting this. What is difficult is trying to figure out what we are supposed to do with what we find, or learn from where we go what will make life even richer. For ourselves, of course. But for the rest of the world, as well.

Deer run, yes, but they never run very far away from the stream at which they drink.

Don't be fooled: Deer run, yes, but they never run very far away from the stream at which they drink. The problem with running through life is that it's possible to outrun our spiritual nourishment. Then we become an empty person in an even emptier place. "The sea is only beautiful," Patrick Field writes, "if there is a shore."

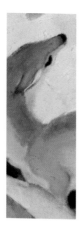

To go through life light-footed—moving quickly from one place to another—does not mean that we go without baggage. We meet ourselves there when we finally arrive; and so, in the end, nothing really changes unless we change it first.

If, when people say "settle down" they mean you should stop reaching for the stars, ignore them. If, on the other hand, they mean know what you want when you say "reach for the stars," as in reach for something worth reaching for, that kind of advice is invaluable. It reminds us that we can't get any-where unless we have a destination in mind.

Life is not meant to be a series of resolutions de-signed to make us someone we're not. It's meant to be a series of explorations which, in the end, finally bring us home to ourselves. "The life so short," Hippocrates says, "the craft so long to learn."

It's not easy to know where you want to be in life. But you can't discover where you're meant to be by simply standing nowhere in particular staring into space. "Life is a process of becoming," Anaïs Nin says, "a combination of states we have to go through. Where people fail is that they wish to elect the state and remain in it. This is a kind of death."

In order to know life, we need to experience life—both its dark and its light sides. Too many of us, perhaps, choose grey. We never risk, so we never fail. But, if truth were told, we never really win either.

Try what you've always wanted to try—secretly, silently, deeply. It has something to teach you about you.

When we arrive at where we're supposed to be in life—where we know that we have finally come home to the fullness of ourselves—there will be no desire to leave it, only the need to plumb it.

It is what we love most to do that makes us ourselves. Then we lose all track of time; then work disappears; then there is nothing but me becoming what I am. The poet William Butler Yeats says of such a state: "O body swayed to music, O brightening glance, how can we know the dancer from the dance?"

There is a magnet in us driving us on to become more of who we really are. The only problem with that is that there is a danger of losing some of who we are as we go, if we have

There is a magnet in us driving us on to become more of who we really are.

not cultivated everything our present state
is meant to develop in us.

Don't
expect
to be
perfect.

Don't expect to be perfect. Failure is built right into
life so that we can learn as we go. Just expect it.
That way you won't be disappointed in yourself.

It's easy to be defensive about what we've done
when we didn't know, to begin with, where we
were going. What a shame. That way we miss the
fun of it. "You grow up," says Ethel Barrymore,
"the first day you have your first good laugh—
at yourself."

Getting stuck in life—refusing to experiment; being
afraid to try something new; becoming cemented
in what is, rather than excited by what could be—is
the difference between living and being alive. "This
is life's greatest moment," Isaac Hecker wrote,
"when the soul unfolds capacities which reach
beyond earth's boundaries."

To become what we are, after years of searching,
hours of learning, and decades, perhaps, of inch-
ing toward the moment when what we know and
what we love to do intersect—it is then that the
fullness of life begins.

Our best gifts do not feel like "gifts" to us. It is other people who must tell us that. All we know is that there is nothing else in life that we can possibly do. As Fred Astaire said when asked why he did what he did, "I have no desire to prove anything by it. I have never used it as an outlet or a means of expressing myself. I just dance."

The best advice we can ever get or give in life is precisely this: "Just dance."

Life is not one dance; it is many. The trick is to move from one to the other with ease and the faith to believe that more are left to come, all of them meant to teach me more than I ever thought I needed or wanted to know.

Getting unstuck in life requires the grace to laugh at both where we've been and where we are, opening ourselves to an outrageous, unthinkable tomorrow. Jean Houston says of that moment, "At the height of laughter, the universe is flung into a kaleidoscope of new possibilities."

Try not to be too serious about life. It is really equivalent to taking a ride on a Ferris wheel, a whirl on a roller coaster

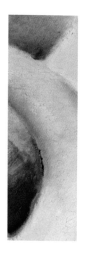

and a couple rounds of dodgems. None of it is without risk, maybe, but all of it is fun.

Deer know that freedom is the capacity to leap the boundaries of life. They teach us, too, that freedom is also the capacity to stay within boundaries when what lies beyond them is more danger than opportunity. "Freedom," Hephzibah Menuhin says, "means choosing your burden."

There is no kind of life that does not bring with it the burdens appropriate to its challenges. All we gain when we change our situations is a new set of burdens. "It came as a shock in life," Anne Morrow Lindberg writes, "to learn that we usually exchange one set of restrictions for another. The second set, however, is self-chosen, and therefore easier to accept."

The function of life is to allow us to discover the scope of the universe within ourselves.

It isn't true that we are where we are because we can't be anywhere else. The real truth is that we are where we are because, for some reason, we do not want to do, to lose, or to attempt what it would take to be somewhere else. And that's fine;

that's freedom. The problem comes when we call that captivity.

Life is not necessarily a smorgasbord of opportunities, but it is a plethora of choices. It's failing to make them, choosing instead simply to slide from one thing to another, that makes the difference. "You don't get to choose how you're going to die. Or when," Joan Baez writes. "You can only decide how you're going to live. Now."

Life is not necessarily a smorgasbord of opportunities but it is a plethora of choices.

There's something you'd like to do in life. Why don't you do it? Really? Is that a good enough reason?

It's not the great decisions of life that determine the emotional quality of our lives. It's the decisions we make day by day that will measure our total happiness quotient as life goes by.

Life is a marathon. Fortunately, running is good for your heart, good for your body, good for your lungs. Yet it's where you're running to—and why—which, in the end, will determine whether you win this race or not.

Running can be dangerous, of course. But to sit down in the middle of life when you should be running is even worse. As some unknown philosopher of life wrote: "Runners just do it—they run for the finish line even if someone else has reached it first."

"The most wasted of all days is one without laughter."

E.e. cummings wrote: "The most wasted of all days is one without laughter." Run through life, head up and laughing. Then life can never defeat you.

Just remember that whatever boundaries you're breaking, they will bring their own challenges with them. Or to put it another way:

Archie: Did you hear about the guy who decided to fly an airplane?

Roy: No, I didn't, Archie, but that's good.

Archie: No, that's bad. He was learning to fly when his airplane caught fire and he had to jump.

Roy: Whoa! That's bad!

Archie: No, that's good. He was wearing a parachute.

Roy: Oh, that's good.

Archie: No, that's bad. The parachute didn't open.

Roy: Oh! That is definitely bad!

Archie: No, that was good. He just happened to jump out right over a farmer's big ol' soft haystack.

14

Roy: Oh! That's good!

Archie: No, that was bad. As he was falling, he spotted a pitchfork in the middle of the haystack.

Roy: Oh-oh! That's bad!

Archie: No, that was good. As it turned out, he missed the pitchfork.

Roy: Now, Archie, I know that's good!

Archie: No, Roy, that wasn't good either. He missed the haystack.

As you begin the New Year, remember that the point is not to win the race. The point is to run the race, fresh and hopeful at every turn, bright and learning at every turn.

ABOUT THE ARTIST

Franz Marc (1880–1916) was a German painter and printmaker, one of the key figures of the German Expressionist movement and a founding member of the journal *The Blue Rider*. Most of his  mature work portrays animals, usually in natural settings. His work is characterized by bright primary color, an almost cubist portrayal of animals, stark simplicity and a profound sense of emotion.

FEBRUARY

HEAD OF A GIRL » BY PAULA MODERSOHN-BECKER » STÄDEL MUSEUM, FRANKFURT AM MAIN

THE AGE OF INNOCENCE

I like children but I don't romanticize them. Children are not necessarily goodness unadulterated. They are goodness in embryo. Childhood calls me to remember what purity was before I had seen evil or violence or cunning or domination in full bloom. Before I myself learned to scheme or hurt.

I do not mourn the loss of innocence. I am more inclined to mourn the loss of the self I was before I began to recognize these things—either in myself or in others. I have come to understand that it is not the unknowing of these things that is virtue. Virtue comes only after we have wrestled with evil or violence and—finally, consciously—turned from them.

So, I smile at images of innocence. There is really no such thing. There are only more or less stages of awareness. I was not innocent—meaning unaware or untouched by the violence around me as a child. I was only powerless to stop it. I am not innocent now about the violence against women in both church and society. Only still powerless to change it.

And yet, I have come to understand that even awareness is its own kind of power, its own kind of innocence. I can, after all, whatever the attempt to convince me of the rightness of oppression in any of its forms, simply refuse to accept it.

Children are not goodness unadulterated. They are goodness in embryo. It is the responsibility of the adults around them to fan that goodness to life.

"Children are the keys of paradise"

"Children are the keys of paradise," Richard Henry Stoddard writes. "They alone are good

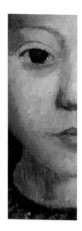

and wise, because their thoughts, their very lives, are prayer." Wrong. The unknowing of evil is not virtue. Virtue comes only after we have wrestled with the corrosion of virtue and finally, consciously, turned from it.

Real innocence is the continuing belief that human beings—we ourselves—are more inclined to care about integrity than we do for money or vengeance or the exploitation of the rest of the human race. It is a commitment to the notion that, in the end, the good in all of us will, eventually, outweigh everything else. And how do we know that? Because we have gone through it ourselves. "Through our recovered innocence," Henry David Thoreau wrote, "we discern the innocence of our neighbors."

There is nothing to be gained by distrust of others except a good dose of paranoia ourselves. The kind that keeps us awake at night.

The innocence of children lies in the fact that they assume innocence in us. "Innocence," Joseph Joubert writes, "is always unsuspicious."

There is something about the innocent that disarms us into remembering the days when we ourselves were more likely, always, to accept the rest of the world with open arms. Maybe that's why the innocent have such a capacity to bring a smile to our faces.

Innocence is the part of a person that accepts what the rest of the world says is impossible, unreliable, unacceptable or false and, far too often, proves the rest of us wrong. "It is innocence that wins and experience that loses," the French poet Péguy writes.

It is the freshness of childhood that makes the mundane delightful.

It's when we allow our experience to smother our innocence that the sense of possibility dies in us and we settle down to become the dust of the ages.

The streak of innocence in us is what makes all things new and enchanting. When that goes, so goes life.

It is the freshness of childhood that makes the mundane delightful, that allows adults to play peekaboo and patty-cake again. Without that we become creatures of argument and caution, reluctant to risk, afraid to enjoy. "Childhood," John

Betjeman writes, "is measured out by sounds and smells and sights, before the dark hour of reason grows."

When we insist that small children act like adults, it is a sure sign that our own adulthood has been bought at too great a price.

The adult is more than reason; the adult is innocence disappointed but wiser as a result.

When disappointment sours us against life rather than teaching us to cultivate other joys, we have robbed ourselves of the only invitation we have to become bigger people than we are at the present moment.

We are meant to outgrow innocence. We are not meant either to scorn it or to devalue it. Rather, innocence outgrown is meant to be the basis of wisdom, the ground of insights about life that carry us from one challenge to the next, that make us capable of risk and full of love of life.

"Childhood," Helen Hayes said, "is a short season." But adulthood is meant to be a long season, and

"Childhood is a short season."

that—without having known the innocence of childhood—is an even more serious problem.

All over the country, all over the world, children are being bought and sold, beaten and killed, abandoned and—worse, perhaps—simply ignored by the very people they depend on for food and care and love and security. We love to think of children as "innocent." But, I thought, as I looked at Modersohn-Becker's "Head of a Girl," are children really innocent—meaning unknowing of evil—or are they simply the silent bearers of the sins adults commit against them? And at what cost—to us as a society—as well as to them?

Dull adults are those who let go of childhood years too quickly. "The aging process," Doug Larson wrote, "has you firmly in its grasp if you never get the urge to throw a snowball."

Don't be afraid to go back and do the things you used to love doing. Better yet, don't be afraid to go forward and find new things you can love doing now. Then, do more of them.

Innocence is the cloth out of which we build our ideals—a true spirit of Christmas; the possibility

of world peace; the security and joy of being a large extended family. As Samuel Ullman says, "Nobody grows old merely by living a number of years. We grow old by deserting our ideals." So don't.

When we can no longer be disappointed in anything, we are no longer really alive. When we are disappointed and refuse to admit it, even to ourselves, we are turning to stone. And that is a possibility even worse than death.

It is possible, just by looking into their eyes, to see a child grow wiser. It is also possible, just by looking into their eyes, to see in older people the eternal youth that makes life beautiful all the way to the end.

The invariable mark of childhood at all ages is the addiction to excess. There is no "enough is enough" in a child. On the other hand, "The first sign of maturity," Jerry M. Wright says, "is the discovery that the volume knob also turns to the left."

Maturity has nothing to do with age. For some, it comes in a childhood hijacked by pain or stimulated by early responsibilities. On the other hand, growing up and growing on are two different things. It is important to make sure that one is not confused with the other. "Age," Tom Stoppard says, "is a high price to pay for maturity."

Innocence and fantasy are not the same things. Accepting life at face value, investing hope in every element of it, is innocence. Fantasy is what refuses to allow life to distinguish between reality and false hope for us.

It is the freshness of child-hood that makes the mundane delightful.

Age may change the body, but if we live it well, it should not ever dampen the soul. That happens only in the mind, whatever the age. "None are so old," Thoreau writes, "as those who have outlived enthusiasm."

Innocence lives in us as long as we get up thinking that today—this day of all days—something wonderful may be about to happen to us and we can hardly wait to see what it will be.

Age is not meant to change what we do. It simply changes the way we do things. Or to put in another way: "Age," Carrie Latet says, "is like the newest version of a software—it has a bunch of great new features but you lose all the cool features of the original version."

"To be seventy years young is sometimes far more cheerful and hopeful than to be forty years old."

The nice thing about growing up is that life gets better, looks better and feels better, the longer time we're at it. "To be seventy years young," Oliver Wendell Holmes wrote, "is sometimes far more cheerful and hopeful than to be forty years old." Be careful. It is so easy to get old, no matter how young we are.

ABOUT THE ARTIST

Paula Modersohn-Becker
(1876–1907) the first German artist to absorb the lessons of French modernism, was one of the most advanced artists of her day, creating a number of groundbreaking images of great  intensity. After her death at the age of 31, she initially became known, not for her art, but for her poignant journals and letters.

MARCH

STILL LIFE WITH FRUIT AND CURTAIN — DETAIL » BY PAUL CÉZANNE » ST. PETERSBURG, HERMITAGE

"Give Us Bread and Roses"

Still-life paintings call to consciousness the stark beauty of what we too often see least, if at all: an old tapestry; a splash of fruit; a once strong barn, perhaps now sunk into ruin, its glory and gain forgotten, its presence overlooked.

At first glance, then, still-life painting does not seem to have much to say to anyone. The subjects they use, in most part, arouse no pathos, provide little in the way of human insight, touch the eye more than the heart. But not this one. Not Cézanne's Still Life with Fruit and Curtain. This one strikes at the core of life. It requires us to ask ourselves what it is that nourishes us. And why.

I, for one, know how easy it is to get caught up in the dramatic and miss the power of the mundane, the wisdom of the daily, the comfort of regularity, the unexciting exciting dimensions of what it means to be really alive. And yet my life cries out for more and more and more of it always.

One week at the desk, one week with the community, one week of quiet commonplace, one week—uninterrupted—soothes my soul beyond any telling of it. The daily schedule nourishes me; the sight of the familiar nourishes me; the silence nourishes me. The banter of friends and the rhythm of prayer, the best of music and the single shaft of promise every new day brings, provide the kind of balm no boughten balm can give.

The question of the painting begs for attention, then: What am I overlooking in life? What nourishes me? Am I doing enough to provide it? What happens to me when I don't?

Whatever the answer to all those things, one thing grows increasingly more obvious as the years pass: every one of us, whoever we are, in this highly frenetic, jangling technological world in which we live—I certainly—needs more of what nourishes us and less of what drains us.

We live in a culture so glutted by multiplicity of people and things that it is almost impossible to appreciate the power of singularity. But, in the end, it is only the singular that has any real effect on us at all. It is in our commitment to the awareness of the singular that we are either nourished or starved of soul.

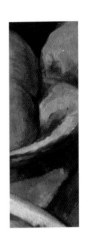

What we concentrate on, the way we spend our time, tells us what we really care about. The whole question is a simple one: How do we spend our time and is that time well-spent where the soul is concerned?

For the most part, modern society is shaped by work rather than by relationships or personal interests. But with that comes the stress and the worry. Shakespeare's advice has been totally forgotten: "Frame your mind to mirth and merriment," he says, "which bars a thousand harms and lengthens life." Not a bad idea in a world where the work never ends and the worry that comes with it never goes away.

There are two ages in life that understand what a gift it is to sit and let the juice of a peach run down your chin. The first is pre-school and the second is retirement. It's the in-between years when the soul goes dry.

When we can't remember how long it's been since we simply sat and looked at something we love, it's been too many months...years....

There is a relationship between good cooking and a good life. Good cooking nourishes relationships, yes, but more than that it nourishes our very zest for all the possibilities of life. "When we no longer have good cooking in the world," Marie-Antoine Careme writes, "we will have no literature, nor high and sharp intelligence, nor friendly gatherings, nor social harmony."

Every human act is an act of nourishment for someone. For others as well as for the self. To plant a tree is to nourish the future. To play good music is to nourish the arts. To read a good book is to nourish the soul.

What we nourish within us determines what we will become. Prayerful or not. Patient or not. Loving or not. "Nourish beginnings," Muriel Rukeyser writes. "Let us nourish beginnings. Not all things are blest, but the seeds of all things are blest. The blessing is in the seed."

Never take anything for granted—the people you
associate with, the things you choose to do in
your free time, the television programs you watch.
Everything touches us, shapes us, nourishes the
thoughts we think. All of them are making us more
or less of what we are meant to be.

It's what we take into ourselves that we then com-
municate to others in some form or other. Maybe
that's what we see in the faces of the holy ones.
What glows so brightly in them is the serenity and
kindness they have nourished within themselves
all their lives.

*We are
all born
grasping
for some-
thing and
spend the
rest of our
lives doing
the same.*

Let life in and you will find more and more of
yourself coming fully alive.

We are all born grasping for something and spend
the rest of our lives doing the same. What we become depends on what we grasp for every minute
of the day. "The pure taste of the apple," Simone
Weil writes, "is as much a contact with the beauty
of the universe as the contemplation of a picture
by Cézanne."

We go through life like robots on an assembly line. Learning to live consciously, to see what we see and to hear what we hear, coaxes the soul into the fullness of its humanity.

Spiritual nourish- ment is anything that fills us with a sense of the fundamen- tal good- ness of life.

When you're sad and mad, depressed and deprived, disappointed and lonely, what nourishes your heart: good tea, fine music, the presence of a friend, a long walk in the rain? Whatever it is, you and you alone can make it happen. And if you don't, you doom yourself to the darkness within.

Spiritual nourishment is anything that fills us with a sense of the fundamental goodness of life, the clear and constant gifting of God.

It is almost impossible to be spiritually nourished in the midst of shapeless, meaningless, soul-searing noise. "True silence," William Penn wrote, "is the rest of the mind, and is to the spirit what sleep is to the body, nourishment and refreshment."

To fail to fill ourselves with good things is to abandon ourselves to useless ones that dry out the center of us and leave us thirsting for the life we were given to cultivate but did not.

No amount of things—no amount of money, no
amount of cars or baubles or parties or houses or
trips—can substitute for being full of life inside
ourselves. "Not what we have," Jean-Antoine Petit-
Senn wrote, "but what we enjoy, constitutes our
abundance."

Good food, fun food, food served in candlelight
or served in the sun—served with a bit of laughter
and a great deal of barely disguised affection—carries us from one chapter in life to another. Carries
us beyond past hurts. Carries us over life's doubts.
Carries us into whole new segments of life. Life
without good food is life without a safety net.
"After a good dinner," Oscar Wilde wrote, "one can
forgive anybody, even one's own relations."

We have become a culture obsessed with eating.
Correction: we are now obsessed with not eating.
Which may well be why we can't stop thinking
about food. As a result, now struggling with the
obsession, we eat more than we should and then
fear to eat the very things that would nourish our
friendships, our memories, our energies for the
rest of life. Good wine, a mother's comfort food,
and a bite of chocolate on a tiring day
become the enemies of our life.
How sad.

Food is the thread of life: We eat at funerals; we eat at weddings; we eat at graduation parties; we eat on holidays. When we are pensive or hurting or lonely or thinking, we begin to look for "comfort food," simple foods that give more warmth to the heart than nourishment for the body. "If you are cold, tea will warm you," William Gladstone said. "If you are heated, it will cool you. If you are depressed, it will cheer you. If you are excited, it will calm you."

Food is the ultimate act of hospitality. It says, I am here to support you, sustain you, share life with you and help you. "The tea pot is on," someone wrote, "the cups are waiting/ Favorite chairs anticipating/ No matter what I have to do/ My friend, there's always time for you." Food is what enables us to open ourselves—unguarded and unboundaried—in ways no other act of life can possibly do.

Nourishment is the medicine of the home. Long before alternative medicines or nutritionists, Hippocrates wrote, "If we could give every individual the right amount of nourishment and exercise, not too little and not too much, we would have found the safest way to health."

When we fail to realize that food is only half the nourishment we need as human beings, we become less a human being than we are meant to be. "Hearts starve as well as bodies," James Oppenheim wrote in a poem honoring women textile strikers. "Give us bread, but give us roses."

We concentrate a lot on providing food for ourselves. But the real question is, How much do we concentrate on providing art for the heart, music for the soul, literature for the mind? "A person should hear a little music, read a little poetry, and see a fine picture every day of life," Johann Wolfgang von Goethe wrote, "in order that worldly cares may not obliterate the sense of the beautiful which God has implanted in the human soul."

Dress up at least once a week.

Dress up at least once a week. Beauty—our own—nourishes a sense of presence in us that overflows into the arenas of life and makes them more beautiful for others, as well.

All the food in the world cannot substitute for the nourishment of the rest of us, the part of us that makes life both livable and human. "Without art, without beauty," Valentin Okorokov wrote, "our life would be poor, dull and unemotional, and it could bring about erosion of the human soul."

Sight is meant to nourish us, so what do we look at?

Sight is meant to nourish us, so what do we look at? Hearing is meant to nourish us, so what do we listen to? Unless we seed the soul with beauty, we cannot possibly live beautiful lives. "All poetry and music, and art of every true sort," J. B. Phillips wrote, "bears witness to our continual falling in love with beauty and our desperate attempt to induce beauty to live with us and enrich our common life."

To be unaware of the soulful in life is to starve the soul. "If you foolishly ignore beauty," the architect Frank Lloyd Wright wrote, "you will soon find yourself without it. Your life will be impoverished."

The longer we live, the more beautiful life becomes. First, we try to control our lives and fail. Then, finally we abandon ourselves to what life gives us and discover how rich we really are.

In the end, what I concentrate on in life will be the measure of the life I live. In the end, it will be beauty, art and the little things of life that nourish us to the end. "Many's the long night," Robert Louis Stevenson wrote, "I dreamed of cheese—toasted, mostly." Point: It's the little things that make life beautiful. Always the little things.

ABOUT THE ARTIST

Paul Cézanne (1839–1906) was a French artist and Post-Impressionist painter whose work laid the foundations of the transition from the 19th-century conception of artistic endeavor to a new and radically different world of art in the 20th century. Cézanne's work demonstrates a mastery of design, color, tone and composition. His often repetitive, sensitive and exploratory brushstrokes are highly characteristic and clearly recognizable.

APRIL

NOCTURNAL BERLIN STREET WITH CAB » BY LESSER URY » ©CHRISTIE'S IMAGES LTD

THE SOLITUDE
OF NIGHT

The problem in this culture may well be that we have destroyed night. Even night is all light and noise and activities now. Where I go to write in a remote village in Ireland for three months of the year, night remains night. There is no light anywhere outside the house; only a few small lights flicker from within the small houses. Inside the house when the turf fire goes out, it is too cold to stay up.

So the dark and the cold set in early and with them an inner life that nothing else nurtures in quite the same way. The loss of night is a loss of human soul, I think, which means that if we do not have it naturally, we need to create it for ourselves: television and computers off, lights out, extra hours of quiet. Then maybe we can find the inside of ourselves again and the voice of God that echoes there so much more clearly than anywhere else.

Life without the solitude that comes with night and the silence that unleashes the self within is a life without serious reflection. It is a life without a soul.

The light bulb gave the world the 24-hour day. Whether or not the world is better off for it is still uncertain. Nothing ever stops anymore. Nighttime has no meaning now. The noise goes on around the clock. So when do we ever really rest? And does that matter?

Having the opportunity to be alone is an important dimension of learning to function alone.

Having the opportunity to be alone is an important dimension of learning to function alone. Having

had the time to define our own personal positions in life we can then go on with the confidence and certainty it takes to know what we think—and then claim it.

"I can't hear myself think," my mother used to say when there was more noise than she could abide. I know now what she meant. The question is, Can anyone hear themselves think in a world steeped in 24 hours of noise? Most of all, what is the effect of that on the level of thinking in this society?

Night blacks out the distractions that divide us from ourselves during the day. It unmasks us to ourselves. "You can live a lifetime," Beryl Markham says, "and, at the end of it, know more about other people than you know about yourself."

When night blocks out the noise and the lights, the mind and the soul come out of hiding and real thinking begins. As the painter Vincent van Gogh said, "I often think that the night is more alive and more richly colored than the day."

Nighttime turns the light on the self. Now there is nothing between me and truth. "There are days," Colette says, "when solitude...is a heady wine that

intoxicates you with freedom...." Then the challenge lies in learning what to do with the freedom.

The solitude of night brings all our fears into focus.
It also gives us the opportunity to trust again in the
coming light of day and the basic awareness that
the universe is friendly and creation is good.

It is solitude that gives us the opportunity to
recover a sense of internal order, to develop new
self-confidence for the day to come, and to experience the spiritual strength it takes for a person,
if necessary, to face tomorrow alone. "I would
rather sit on a pumpkin and have it all to myself,"
Henry David Thoreau writes, "than be crowded
on a velvet cushion."

"I would rather sit on a pumpkin and have it all to myself, than be crowded on a velvet cushion."

For those for whom one day blurs into another
with dizzying speed, night brings with it a re-
newed sense of self and the courage it takes to go
on dealing with the clamor that comes with any
highly-active life.

The modern world seems to assume that anyone
who prefers quiet to noise is antisocial—or worse.
The real truth may simply be that the person
who can be alone is healthy enough, self-assured

enough, to like their own company. "What a commentary on our civilization," Anne Morrow Lindbergh wrote, "when being alone is considered suspect, when one has to apologize for it, make excuses, hide the fact that one practices it—like a secret vice." Commentary: What "civilization"?

There are two distinctly different spiritual parts of the day—night and day. Each of them shows us a different face of God and a different image of the self. Coming to understand one is key to understanding the other.

When we cultivate silence, we are really cultivating communication.

Solitude gives us the self-knowledge it takes to trust ourselves, even in a crowd that would like it better if we were like them rather than uniquely us. "In solitude," Laurence Sterne says, "the mind gains strength and learns to lean upon itself."

When we cultivate silence, we are really cultivating communication. Silence teaches us to listen—to ourselves and even to others.

Night is one way to learn solitude; being surrounded by strangers is another. Busses, metros, airplanes, waiting rooms plunge us into the very center of ourselves. They are a gift to the soul in the middle of a hectic day. Edith Wharton writes of it, "She was not accustomed to taste the joys of solitude except in company."

Solitude is not a deprivation; it soothes the nerves and quiets the mind and gives us respite from the unending jabber of useless conversations.

Night is the first line of therapeutic defense for those exhausted by the demands for attention that come with the day.

Night itself does not release a string of prayers. Night is a prayer. It is the beginning of the communion that comes with a sense of the uninterrupted presence of God in life.

It is in the stillness of night that we really open ourselves to the world, to our inner selves and to the relationship between them. "The dead of moonlight," Anna Letitia Barbauld writes, "is the noon of thought."

Without solitude we run the risk of losing touch with ourselves and what we really think, what is

really important to us, who we really are under all the guises of the day. Night is meant to be where we can most be ourselves, where we can come to know and heal ourselves from the strain of trying to be what others want us to be.

In large groups, we lose a part of ourselves to the will of the crowd. But when we are alone, we become who we really are.

We spend far too much time thinking about who we will be in the group and far too little time thinking about who we really are when we are alone. It is the relationship between the two that is the measure of the human being's integrity.

The African proverb says, "The earth is a beehive; we all enter by the same door but live in different cells." To lose touch with the separated self is to become a figment of the group mind. But bifurcated, divided in two, is not who we were born to be.

The language has a new phrase for this inner/outer struggle of the self for wholeness: "Get it together." When what we really mean is bring your outer self, your presentation of self to the group, in line with your awareness of who you really are inside.

"We enter this life naked and alone," Thomas De Quincey wrote, "and we leave it the same way." The only question then is, What kind of person are we in between those times—independent and strong of mind or dependent on others and unsure of ourselves? It takes silence and solitude to really know the answer to that question.

The great by-product of solitude is self-containment, the secret power of an inner strength honed from self-knowledge and self-esteem.

When solitude teaches us who we are, we no longer need the affirmation of others. We are no longer beholden to public approval, because we have developed a firm foundation for our own.

When solitude teaches us who we are, we no longer need the affirmation of others.

Humility grows in the dark of night out of the insight that comes with solitude. "We are rarely proud," Voltaire writes, "when we are alone."

When we know who we are, when we have confronted the spirits within ourselves against which we vie for dominance, we find ourselves more inclined to be so much kinder to everyone else.

Learning silence and solitude, learning to love solitude and rest in silence, is the beginning of freedom and independence. "When you close your doors and make darkness within," Epictetus wrote, "remember never to say that you are alone, for you are not alone; nay, God is within and your genius is within."

ABOUT THE ARTIST

Lesser Ury (November 7, 1861—October 18, 1931) was a German Impressionist painter and printmaker. His subjects were landscapes, urban land-scapes, and interior scenes, treated in an Impressionistic manner that ranged from the subdued tones of figures in a darkened interior to the effects of streetlights at night to the dazzling light of foli-age against the summer sky.

MAY

ON THE BEACH — DETAIL » WINSLOW HOMER » NEW YORK, COLLECTION FORBES

OF DREAMS
AND MEMORIES

Like the boys in Homer's "On the Beach" I spent a great deal of time as a child sitting on the bluff overlooking Lake Erie staring across to Canada, dreaming of what it must be like to see other lands and to live the way other people lived.

But most of all, I spent the time thinking about my own life and its future.

The problem was that I didn't know then the difference between a dream and a plan. A plan is a strategy; a dream is an idea.

The distinction between the two is subtle but determining. The fact is that without dreams, no plans are possible.

Whatever happens to the pastiche of dreams that live and change and fade away in the young me—a desire to see the world, or fly an airplane, or be an athlete—it is the dream that dominates my life that really counts.

Dreams are not plans. Dreams are destinations toward which we bend our lives, not possibilities unfulfilled. The dream of becoming the fullness of myself drives me from yesterday to tomorrow—not stuck in memory, impervious to today, an invitation to a future yet in process. Dreams are the life blood of becoming. When I stop dreaming, a level of what it means to be alive ends in me, as well.

A plan is within my control; a dream is hope in the mist. I hope to go around the world; I hope for an education, a job, someone to love, something to save me from what is. Dreams show me the quality of my ideals. It is the willingness to dream on, to dream higher, to pursue a dream that enables me to live beyond "what is" for "what could be."

In every dream lurks the bittersweet siren call of "perhaps," and "if only," and "because," and "I must." They carry me on angels' wings from one time to another, however impossible either past or future may seem. But dreams are not certainties; they are the ideals by which we live our lives.

The difficulty with dreams is that if we suppress them we may live to regret the present. The worst of all possibilities is to go through life mourning the dreams we never pursued.

At the same time, if we refuse to adjust our dreams to the reality in which we live, we may fail to see how much of what we want we have really achieved. The function of a dream is to give life a direction, not to give it pain. It is the difference between "I always wanted something like this..." and "I wish I had tried...."

It all depends on us.

MAY

In South Pacific, one of the longest running Broadway musicals of all time, Bloody Mary sings "If you don't have a dream, how you gonna have a dream come true?" It's a life lesson far beyond the philosophy of life we have come to expect from the average musical. The truth is that it is the goals we nurture within us that determine the eventual quality of our lives. If we aspire to less than we can be, we will get exactly that.

If we aspire to less than we can be, we will get exactly that.

Our dreams are lodged in our memories so that no matter how troubled life may be at any single moment, we can never forget that we are going in the direction of something more than whatever this is. Memory, the dreams of what can be, has kept people alive in every kind of captivity and degradation. "God gave us memories," J.M. Barrie wrote, "that we might have roses in December."

Dreams drive us beyond what is to what we seek. It is fanning our dreams, defining what we seek, that will eventually take us to where they are real.

Dream big but realize that every great hope is achieved one small step at a time along the way.

The best of our memories are the life blood of our dreams: the smell of fresh bread, the sight of a fishing rod, the feel of a cheap, small trophy. They all measure the goodness of our lives, both past and present. Whatever it is that evokes contentment in us, it is precisely those things we most seek.

Our memories hold for us the images of everything we most desire in life, the specter of everything we most avoid.

"We do not remember days, we remember moments," Cesare Pavese tells us. It is the gemstone of singular memories that store in symbol for us the sum total of the real hopes and fears of our lives. It is out of such things that our dreams are shaped and reshaped.

MAY

What we remember in life, and have learned
from, constitutes the volume of wisdom in us. To
the degree we find meaning in what we remember, to that degree we are wise as well as clever.
To that degree every day is a better day for us.

No amount of intelligence learned in a classroom
is equal to one ounce of wisdom distilled from my
memories.

Imagination and memory are not the same things.
Imagination is derived from memory. Because of
what we remember, we either build a better world
for ourselves or we replicate what we did not learn
from in a sad past.

"The past is never dead," William Faulkner wrote.
"It is not even past." But if that is true, then we
never escape the past because it lives in us forever.
But there is one thing we can do: We can refuse to
allow it to go on controlling us. We can live into the
dream of a better present because of it.

*The size
of our
futures
depends
on the
size of our
dreams.*

The size of our futures depends on the size
of our dreams.

*Our
dreams
are the
path to
a new kind
of present.*

Our dreams are the path to a new kind of present. They not only show us what we seek; they show us what it will take to get there. Most of all, they make the length and difficulty of the journey worthwhile.

It never hurts to dream of the desirable; it always hurts never to dream of it at all. Beyond where we are is the rest of us, the unfinished us, the incomplete us. It takes the dream of more to get us there.

Sometimes what we want to forget is as important to the creation of a new dream as anything we could possibly remember. As the essayist Montaigne says, "Nothing fixes a thing so intensely in the memory as the wish to forget it."

Every dream that becomes a reality is the beginning of a new one.

Life is the pursuit of one dream after another until all the possibilities in us are exhausted and life takes on the shape we give it. Clearly, it is the dreams we make for ourselves that determine the life we live.

If our dreams of the future are born out of our past, then time is the seedbed of the future. It is what we have come from that charts the way to the future.

It is important to remember, as Anne Morrow Lindbergh writes, "Duration is not a test of true or false." Just because something in our lives has gone on and on for years does not mean that it must always be. Whatever is not good is up to us either to change or to learn to live with better than we have.

We so often mistake the nature of time. We act as if it were a line behind us when, as a matter of fact, it is the pool of life that is within us. It is what we draw from the pool of yesterday that will determine the choices we need to make tomorrow if tomorrow is to be better than the past.

The past cannot be solved by pretending to forget it. There is no such thing. Time is a permanent mark on our souls. What is not permanent is the way in which we deal with it.

If we assume that what we have been we must always be, we have forgotten—or never knew—the

power of a dream to put new energy into making life new again.

To defer the dream of my life—to put off doing what needs to be done if I am ever to become the fullness of myself, to assume that there is time to do tomorrow what should have been done a lifetime of yesterdays ago—is to defy the natural process of life. It is also to deny the very purpose of my life. Simone Weil puts it this way, "Time does us violence; it is the only violence."

We rush through life; we throw our dreaming times away or fill them to the rim with the mundane or the useless. And with them goes the opportunity to dream a better way to live the little time we have.

We fill time with things that rob us of the very time we covet to live life well. We forget to take the time to think, to stop, to dream, to breathe, to look, to try something new. "Killing time," Karen Elizabeth Gordon says, "takes practice."

A visitor to the office of a very successful business saw a man sitting at a window, head back against the high leather neck rest of his chair, feet up on his desk, hands crossed on his chest, staring into space. "You see that guy there," the visitor said. "He's doing nothing but sitting around thinking." The owner cast a sharp look at the visitor and then said tersely, "He better be. That's what I pay him for."

Absolutely nothing new could possibly happen in the world if it weren't for its dreamers. So why do we put so much energy into insisting that people be busy all the time?

We teach students to calculate, and compute, and memorize, and recite. When do we ever teach them to dream?

When we take the time to wonder what life would be like if something common to it—like schools or banks or churches—disappeared, we are suddenly free to dream of living differently. Then, the question is an obvious one: Would that be better or worse?

When we don't take time to dream about what we might want to do next in life, we are too busy to be alive.

Absolutely nothing new could possibly happen in the world if it weren't for its dreamers.

Efficiency and logic have never been what enabled us to see life differently.

A traveling salesman, seeing a farmer holding a large pig up to an apple tree to feed him an apple, stopped and asked, "Wouldn't it save a lot of time just to pick the apple yourself and give it to the pig?" And the farmer replied, "Ah, don't worry about it. After all, what's time to a pig?" Efficiency and logic have never been what enabled us to see life differently, to imagine another way of being alive, to try what has never been tried before us, if for no other reason than to see if it works.

ABOUT THE ARTIST

Winslow Homer (February 24, 1836–September 29, 1910) was an American landscape painter and print-maker, best known for his marine subjects. Largely self-taught, Homer began as a commercial illustra-tor. Later he took up oil painting, producing major works characterized by their weight and density. He also worked extensively in watercolor, primarily chronicling his working vacations.

JUNE

IRISES — DETAIL » BY VINCENT VAN GOGH » LOS ANGELES, J. PAUL GETTY MUSEUM

LOOK! ONE
WHITE IRIS

There is something about van Gogh's riot of irises in *a wild meadow that captures a freeze-frame of life for me. Like that one cluster of blue among a multitude of orange, like that one white iris on the edge of the frame, I am always immersed in something beautiful. But none of it is the totality of life. It is all only a small and transient sliver of it, struggling for breath in the crush of the rest of it. It's all alluring and all momentary; it's all worthwhile and all transitory. And when it's over, I realize that I had very little time to look at any of it completely.*

We rush from one thing to another and wonder why we don't remember where we've been or what we've done or whom we met there. Or worse yet, we go from one thing to another so fast we have no idea what was there, pressed in the midst of it that we never even saw.

Indeed, life is a meadow of irises crushed by the plenty of the beauty around them. It's learning to look for one white iris everywhere we are that will, in the end, save the soul from the confusion of abundance.

"Great things are not done by impulse but by a series of small things brought together."

Life is made up of small things—single incidents, separate questions, distinct events, one person at a time. One of life's greatest gifts is knowing how to give the self to each of them as they appear rather than allow any of them to blur into nothingness. It is learning to be present to where we are and what we're doing that gives life substance. As Vincent van Gogh said, "Great things are not done by impulse but by a series of small things brought together."

To see one blade of grass at a time rather than simply a mountainside of green makes every element of life important.

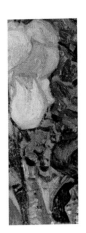

Beauty lies in the consciousness of singularity, not in imageless profusion.

"If you've seen one, you've seen them all" is the underlying untruth of life. It turns life into a short list of categories rather than expanding it into an endless list of surprises.

We ourselves are not here simply as "humans" or "females" or "males" or as "Arabs" or "Americans" or as "bus drivers" or "professors." We are here as ourselves. Only ourselves. And we want to be seen as that. Anything less than that disfigures us, as we disfigure those to whom we ourselves are tempted to do the same.

Confronting and accepting uniqueness is the essence of what it means to be one human being in relationship with another.

It is coming to see life around us in all its singleness, all its particularity, each element of its stun-

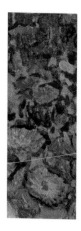

ning selfness, that fills the soul with more beauty than sadness or pain can ever eclipse.

The spiritual life is more than doctrine. It is coming to see God in the works of God. "The losing of Paradise," the Indian Rabindranath Tagore wrote, "is enacted over and over again by the children of Adam and Eve. We clothe our souls with messages and doctrines and lose the touch of the great life in the naked breast of nature."

Realize that mysticism is the gift of learning to see Life under life, behind life, and beyond life. At that stage we have come to see fully. We stop stumbling through life and begin to walk there carefully and thoughtfully.

Nature teaches us many things. It is coming to hear this language, that is beyond language, which is the language of the soul.

Spring teaches us patience. Things—and we, as well—grow slowly. Do not overvalue the speed that races to produce what the heart is not yet wise enough to use well.

Summer teaches us that to have the fullness of life—great tastes, good fun, warm sun and wild abandon—we must have less of it than we expect. Too much of anything sears the soul.

Fall teaches us the value of resting our minds as well as our bodies, the value of readiness, the value of transition. In all the in-between phases and places of life, we are given the time to allow our souls to catch up with our restless energies, to take stock of the present, to get sight of all our possible futures and choose between them.

Winter teaches us what it means to close one phase of life so that we can begin something else, totally different, totally new. It gives us the joy of beginning over and over again throughout the whole of life.

To live in rhythm with the seasons was natural in an agri-cultural society.

To live in rhythm with the seasons was natural in an agricultural society. Now, in the technologi-cal age, it has become a spiritual discipline, a sign of maturity yet to be developed. Ralph Waldo Emerson wrote, "Adopt the pace of nature: her secret is patience."

Everything that grows in us in life is an experience from which we are meant to grow. But everything that grows in us does not have equal value. The question is: what is growing in you right now? What is it doing to your best self? Is it to be nurtured or excised? "Most things come and go, however good to watch. A few things stay and matter to the end," Reynolds Price says. "Rain, for instance."

Like the meadows and trees around us, we are meant to become the fullness of ourselves.

Like the meadows and trees around us, we are meant to become the fullness of ourselves. But that takes reflection and discernment, passion and purpose. It is a matter of knowing what is in us and bringing it to fullness. It is more a matter of becoming than of wishing. The Chinese say, "A human must stand with mouth open for a long time before a roast duck flies in."

It is insignificance that has become significant now. Once we thought of ourselves as the rulers of the universe, the crown of creation, the ultimate and only fully living thing. Now, thanks to space travel, we have come to see ourselves in all our insignificance, as well. We know now that we are only part of creation and certainly not its rulers. As Neil Armstrong, US astronaut put it, "It suddenly struck me (in the space capsule) that that tiny pea, pretty and blue, was the Earth. I put up my thumb and shut one eye and my thumb blotted out the planet Earth.

I didn't feel like a giant. I felt very, very small."
Finally, the sense of superiority that led us to attempt to conquer space—and so instead discover
our smallness—has brought us the humility that
can make us all better citizens of the Earth.

The human quest for conquest ends only in the
awareness of the need to conquer the arrogance
of the self. "Laws change;" Abraham Lincoln
wrote, "people die; the land remains." When we
learn that, ecology will be a given, not a hope.

When we see things only en masse, in great, large,
sweeping entities, we lose the mystery of life. "The
moment one gives close attention to anything,
even a blade of grass," Henry Miller writes, "it
becomes a mysterious, awesome, indescribably
magnificent world in itself."

There is a call to nature in all of us—the challenge
of the mountains, the enormity of the ocean, the
cry of the clouds, the stolidity of the trees—that
both calls us beyond ourselves and into ourselves.
Each of them is already in us, one more powerful
than the other, attempting to teach us what we
need to know.

Water calls us to explore the depth of the self. It washes away, wave after wave, the seismic shocks of the day upon our souls. It soothes the riled self.

Fire drives us out of ourselves. It touches the spark within us that leads us to create new worlds in the face of the years gone to ashes before us.

Earth, the vast expanse of the plains, the colors in a far away meadow, beckons us to explore, to know, to touch, to grow with the environment around us. It makes us its own and teaches us what home is about.

Air, fresh and soft, teaches us how little it takes to live, to go on, to be pure of heart, to begin to live all over again, to believe. "The whole earth," Mohammad said, "has been made a mosque and pure for me."

What nature has to teach us, if we will only take the time in this technological world to listen, is the very rhythm and richness of life. "Climb the mountains...," John Muir writes. "Nature's peace will flow into you as sunshine flows into trees. The winds will blow their own freshness into you, and the storms their energy, while cares will drop off like autumn leaves."

We live, most of us, in a boxed-in world, secure from the wind, away from the water, shaded from the sun, free from the rain, cemented a distance from the woods. We live totally unnatural lives and wonder why we feel out of place here. "Come forth into the light of things," William Wordsworth writes in another age. "Let Nature be your teacher."

We write a lot about nature but we do very little in this age to pursue it.

We write a lot about nature but we do very little in this age to pursue it. We live with light bulbs that eliminate night rather than with telescopes to explore it. "What humbugs we are," Logan Pearsall Smith writes, "who pretend to live for Beauty and never see the Dawn!"

We are blind and do not know it. Deaf and do not care. Spiritless we talk about spirituality. Only those who look and listen ever really find God here. "A prisoner lived in solitary confinement for ten years," Anthony de Mello tells. "He saw and spoke to no one, and his meals were served through an opening in the wall. One day, an ant came to his cell. The man contemplated it in fascination as it crawled around the room. He held it in the palm of his hand the better to observe it, gave it a grain or two....It suddenly struck him that it had taken him ten long years of solitary confinement to open his eyes to the loveliness of an ant."

ABOUT THE ARTIST

Vincent van Gogh (1853–1890) born in Groot-Zundert, Holland, was a post-Impressionist painter whose work had a far-reaching influence on later art for its vivid colors and emotional impact. Van Gogh's finest works were produced in less than three years in a technique that grew more and more impassioned in brushstroke, in symbolic and intense color, in surface tension, and in the movement and vibration of form and line.

JULY

THE HOUSE OF CARDS — DETAIL » BY CHARLES HUNT » NEW YORK, COLLECTION FORBES

ON YOUR MARK,
GET SET, PLAY

The British painter Charles Hunt knew something about life that he apparently also knew was worth passing on in vivid, soft and whimsical imagery, in images that stick to the soul. In his famous work *The House of Cards*, Hunt teases us with it. At first, the painting seems to be nothing more than a kind of domestic snapshot. Until we look again. There, behind the placid rendition of children playing, Hunt's oil painting gives us a variation of what has become one of life's givens: "the family that prays together, stays together," we say. True enough. But Hunt puts a parallel point on the essence of what it means to have a happy life. He paints for the world to see: "the family, the group, the couple, the persons that play together, stay together."

In a highly-productive consumer society, it is a lesson dearly to be learned.

Here we see again what far too many of us forgot far too long ago: there is something about taking the time to do nothing important that is important. Play washes ambition out of the soul. Instead, it is about doing something simply for the pure joy of doing it. For one brief moment in the midst of striving to stay alive, there is no product to be produced, no personal gain to be sought, nothing to prove. That may be why childhood is so largely devoted to play, to the exhilaration of aimlessness. It is the one period in life when we are allowed to wallow in the understanding that just being alive is enough for us. No money or medals needed. No evaluations expected. No better or worse implied.

Play releases the mind to think outside the boundaries of both the self and the society that shapes us. It teaches us the joy of freedom and gives us the right to break all the rules: we can dirty our shoes, laugh out loud, slide in the grass and blow bubbles to nowhere, and no one will care. It enables us to stop taking ourselves too seriously, an insight of eternal importance if we are to live well with others and be able to bear our own failures later when being able to fail becomes our greatest success in life.

We learn, too, that, in the end, life is itself a "house of cards" built to collapse—however much the strain or tension, skill or concentration we give it as we go. Play exposes us to the fact that there is nothing we ever do in life, however high we go in the process, that is permanent. Only

that simple lesson itself is permanent. And, in the end, that may well
be enough to carry us calmly and expectantly from one of life's games
to the next.

JULY

To develop a sense of play in life makes life a great
deal more playful for everyone around us. What
we have to bring to it then makes life less a burden
and more a joy.

Those who cannot play cannot begin to find all the
energy they really need to work. The irony of over-
work is that it makes good work impossible.

Real play is not something that is meant to be done
once a year, let alone once a lifetime.

Learning how to play is one of life's most important skills. It takes a lot of practice, like weekly at
least, to get the full benefit of it in our lives.

Play is not "relaxation." It is the active endeavor to
live differently than the way we do when we work.

When we learn to play better, we learn to love better, too. We become easier to live with, better to be

around, more creative when we work, more full of the joy of life always.

Play doesn't take money; it takes a commitment to do what we like to do at the lowest level possible. It doesn't take a yacht to go fishing; it takes a pole. "We all have our plaything," Lady Mary Wortley Montagu wrote. "Happy are those who are contented with those they can obtain."

It is so easy to do nothing and think we're playing. But playing develops a new way to experience life in us, while doing nothing just leaves us where we were when we started. "It is better," Confucius said, "to play than to do nothing."

Play is the fresh air of the soul.

Play is the fresh air of the soul. It is meant to enliven us. It is meant to renew our energies regularly. It is the recess of life.

Play is not useless activity. It is the activity that frees us to be the rest of ourselves. "You can discover more about a person," Plato said, "in an hour of play than in a year of conversation."

To watch a person play is to see what no other
activity in life can show us about them.

Beware the person who cannot play. They live
in a dark room in a deep cave at the bottom of
themselves. They have little capacity for helping
others to survive the twists and turns of life in
good mental health and with the creativity it takes
to deal with what's coming next.

"If animals play," Susanna Miller writes, "it is
because play is useful in the struggle for survival.
It practices and so perfects the skills needed in
adult life." It is in play that we learn to abandon
ourselves to what is possible, to what is fanciful—
both of them windows to new ways to be alive.

Games give us the chance to develop the parts of
ourselves that nothing else in life ever calls out of
us but which we may sometime need on a moment's notice.

Play allows us to make mistakes that are not
mistakes, just other ways to do what, in the real
world, we are not allowed to try. "Play," Diane
Ackerman teaches, "is our brain's favorite way of
learning."

Not only must we learn to play ourselves, we must be sure that the people who work with us have time to play, as well. If we want to succeed in a highly creative and technological world, we must give people the opportunity to try out new ways of doing things. Then, what we all do together will be even more effective. "If you want creative workers," John Cleese wrote, "give them enough time to play."

Play puts joy where before only pressure had been. And joy puts energy into what would otherwise be pure routine.

If you want to think differently, live differently. If you want to produce better, play more.

Dr. Leila Denmark retired at 103 as America's oldest practicing physician. She says of play, "Anything on earth you want to do is play. Anything on earth you have to do is work. Play will never kill you but work will. I have never worked a day in my life." Make all of life fun. Make all your work a game.

Play gives us a chance to try new things: to build a house out of ice, to make a yard out of sand, to

make chess the measure of what it means to lose
well and then try again. When we know how to
play, we know how to keep trying new ways to do
what we must do anyway. "Play," Einstein said, "is
the highest form of research."

What wears us down is not the work we do; it is
the way we do it. To work without engaging in
play with great exuberance and serious regularity is to jeopardize the very things we want to do
best.

*What
wears us
down is not
the work
we do; it
is the way
we do it.*

Every day take an hour to do what you love to
do, and you won't be able to work fast enough or
hard enough to get there soon enough to do it.

Play is a talent adults understood as children
and then need to develop again later in life, if for
no other reason than to make getting up in the
morning an exciting event.

Play sets the mind, the soul, the heart and the
spirit free. Not to play is not to live fully. The fullness of life depends on the joy of life as well as
the productivity of life. "The highest existence,"
Conrad Hyers writes, "is not work. The highest
existence is play."

Play is the impulse of the soul towards newness. "The creation of something new is not accomplished by the intellect," Carl Jung writes, "but by the play instinct acting from inner necessity. The creative mind plays with objects it loves."

To create something new, simply present the mind with the project, the problem, the question, the purpose. Then play a bit. Do something else, something you enjoy. Let the mind alone, force nothing, and let it play, too.

Children are the only people in the family who let grandparents play and look busy at the same time.

Play is of the essence of the happy life. It is not something we ignore as we grow older. It is something we finally learn to appreciate as we grow older. "We don't stop playing because we grow old," according to George Bernard Shaw. "We grow old because we stop playing."

Children and grandparents make great partners. Children are the only people in the family who let grandparents play and look busy at the same time. Play keeps us alive. It opens us to the surprises of life. It makes people stop and think "At her age!" Which is, of course, the most meaningful thing anyone can ever say about us. Or as Katharine Hepburn put it: "If you obey all the rules, you miss all the fun."

I remember the very first time—years ago—that I saw retirees in Florida riding their bikes—in shorts! It changed my life. And definitely for the better. Try it sometime.

You're not creative? You don't know anybody who's creative? You have no idea what it means to play? Let alone be creative? Take Robert Fulghum's advice: "If you want an interesting party sometime, combine cocktails and a fresh box of crayons for everyone." Good luck, good living, good life.

ABOUT THE ARTIST

Charles Hunt (1829–1900) was a British painter of often humorous and historical subjects. He exhibited at the Royal Academy from 1862–1873. A relatively unknown artist, he painted modern life in the 1850s. He is best known now for his Irish cottage scenes and many pictures of children's games.

AUGUST

AT THE PIANO » BY HERBERT MASARYK » PRAG, NATIONAL (NARODNI) GALERIE

OUR UNPLAYED
MELODIES

Masaryk's At the Piano leaves a haunting feeling in its wake. The large empty room, the silent keys, the dark tones tell of times past, times over, times lost, times unfinished, unknown times ahead. Who of us hasn't known them all?

The only question is whether or not we come to see the unplayed melodies of our lives as enriching for us as were all the themes we played before them.

Music, for instance, had always been a hiding place for me. To this day, I often regret the loss of it. And yet, I also came to realize, there is an even deeper impact of it on my life than the loss of it alone.

Having to leave my piano behind when we left one part of Pennsylvania to settle in another was a great rupture in my young life. I was only ten years old when it happened but, more than anybody knew, to lose the piano was to lose my whole world. I had learned as an only child to make the piano my friend, my companion, my refuge.

On the other hand, I finally came to realize that to have found a new life and new possibility in my new world was itself a gift. There was a whole new world to be explored.

In the end, then, there's no doubt that it was the very loss of music that finally catapulted me into writing. And most ironic of all, it was learning to pattern my sentences on the rhythm and structures of the various musical genres—the march, the waltz, the concerto, allegro or andante, dolce or forza—that forged my writing and speaking style.

Now there's the rub: Was music, then, really a loss or not? Or was the loss of music what really moved me to where I was actually meant to be? "God writes straight in crooked lines," the Portuguese say.

The problem is that it can take a lifetime to learn the full implications of that very simple insight—to come to trust today, to look forward to every unexpected tomorrow. To ask ourselves at every turn, at every moment of choice, what is most important in life right now? What really fits? Because whatever the answer to those two questions, is the answer to the direction of my life.

Life is a series of different melodies, all sung separately but each, in the end, essential to its theme.

"Music expresses that which cannot be put into words and that which cannot remain silent."

"Music," Victor Hugo wrote, "expresses that which cannot be put into words and that which cannot remain silent." Like music, life is made up of both spoken and unspoken elements. Getting the right relationship between the two is what makes it beautiful.

All the moments of emptiness, of silence, of apparent uselessness in life are only launching points for a future yet unknown. The trick is to accept them for what they are: the time out of time that it takes to allow the soul to catch up with the body.

Music is made up of chords and melodies, crescendos and decrescendos, each of which adds to the texture of the piece. Life, too, is made up of alternate moods and opposite rhythms, all designed to hone in us the fullness of character for which we strive.

Don't ever wish for a quiet life. Without turmoil we can never completely learn who we really are.

There's no way to grow without growing. Or as Angelina Jolie says, "The only way to have a life is to commit to it like crazy."

In every life we choose both the notes we'll sing and the melody we give them. Some people complain about everything; some people complain about nothing. "Our life," Marcus Aurelius said, "is what our thoughts make it."

To live well it is not necessary to do one thing only. What is necessary is to do what is most important for both myself and for the rest of the world.

What we think we want to do may not be what we most need to do to complete the growing of the self. "Talent develops in quiet places," Johann Wolfgang von Goethe wrote, "character in the full current of human life."

To complete the song of our lives, we must be willing to sing it always and to the end. "A life without a cause," Barbarella writes, "is a life without effect."

The music of my life drips into the soul, low and dolorous, high and excited, until finally, we come

to hear the song we're meant to sing. Then, it won't matter if anyone else hears it or not.

It is so easy to get lost in the arpeggios of life and miss its melody completely. "Our life," Henry David Thoreau taught, "is frittered away by detail. Simplify. Simplify." Don't get trapped spending the joy of it on either the frivolous or the inconvenient.

All of life is an empty room. It is our task to fill it with something worth listening to.

It is one thing to do things in life; it is another to make whatever we do have meaning for someone else.

The good we do for others becomes the audience of our souls.

To spend a life weighed down by fear of playing a wrong note is to miss the beauty of the rest of the concerto.

How do I know if I'm playing as well as others, better than most? Easy. It all depends on whether or not I'm being true to my best self. Or as Friedrich Nietzsche puts it: "You have your way. I have my way. As for the right way, the correct way, and the only way, it does not exist."

We are not meant to spend our lives playing only in empty rooms. We are put here to help others make their lives beautiful, too.

They're taking art out of schools so they'll have more money to build bombs and put more people in highrise apartment buildings. And they wonder why we don't have soul enough to save our own inner cities.

If we would teach children beauty, the desperation this culture breeds could end over night.

Everyone has something important to do in life.

When the darkness of life smothers the song in you, sing even more loudly so that others can hear another melody and follow it.

Everyone has something important to do in life. Right now. Here. Be faithful to the song within you so that its passion can call forth the song of others as well.

It's common for people to make a living. It's rare for people to make a life. And this culture proves it.

Down deep everybody wants to do some one big thing in life. Few ever really get to do what they most want to do. But so what? It's the wanting that makes life, life. "Go confidently," Thoreau writes, "in the direction of your dreams."

The only mistake a musician can make is to fail to play the instrument they've been given.

Each of us has come to give the world a concert. But how? Marva Collins says, "Trust yourself. Think for yourself. Act for yourself. Speak for yourself. Be yourself. Imitation is suicide." The answer rings true.

The only mistake a musician can make is to fail to play the instrument they've been given. When we refuse to make out of every day the best day it can possibly be, we let the entire world down. As Andy Offutt Irwin says, "Don't be afraid to be amazing."

Life is not about knowing exactly what we're meant to do. It's about doing what must be done that makes of our lives a song.

Learning to see the world differently, to appreciate it newly, to live in it with inner ease, is to make beautiful music out of straw.

The only thing that stands to defeat us is the need to do something that someone else has decided we should do. "The minute you begin to do what you want to do," R. Buckminster Fuller says, "it's really a different kind of life."

All of life is meant to be a recital for the audience that is myself. When I play that one well, I will unleash a symphony of possibility in the imagination of those around me.

No pianist plays beautiful music without practicing for years. Never let either fear or failure stop you from beginning over and over again. Then, some day, you will come to understand that life is not about being perfect. It is simply about being willing to keep trying until we become what we seek.

ABOUT THE ARTIST

Herbert Masaryk (1880–1915) was a painter in the Art Nouveau style. A reaction to academic art of the 19th century and to the drab, boring functionality of the industrial revolution, Art Nouveau is a philosophy of design which made art—from architecture and furniture to paintings—part of ordinary life.

SEPTEMBER

THE GLEANERS » BY JEAN-FRANÇOIS MILLET » PARIS, MUSÉE D'ORSAY

THE GIFT
OF WORK

At first glance, Millet's The Gleaners, an oil painting from the height of the mid-19th century's Second Industrial Revolution, seems pastoral, bucolic, unthreatening. But look again. There are two very powerful, very contentious, ideas on a collision course here.

The first idea comes from an echo of Scripture's book of Ruth. There Ruth, a young widow, supports herself and her mother-in-law by collecting the leftovers in the field after the harvest is finished. The scene is a common one to the Jewish mind, an act of community, mandated by the Torah itself.

The second idea, and the reason for which Millet's painting was rejected at that time in history, is because the industrialists of the period were more interested in making money than in doing compassion.

To this day, the purpose of work has more to do with getting rich than with making the world a better place to live in.

In the West people learn to work so that eventually they won't need to work at all. Work has become a burden in this society, a curse, a sign of social diminishment on those who need to work in order to live. Success in this society belongs to those who don't have to work. Instead, their money makes money. What a pity. Not only for their own sense of self but also pitiful for those whose work is not sufficient to sustain human dignity.

As a result, we stand to lose the whole sense of work as our gift to the world. Most of us are so far removed from the end product of what we do that we have no idea what it really is or how it affects the people who receive it. We make screws—and never know if they're for cruise missiles or artificial heart pumps.

In generations before us, the work people did went straight into the mouths of children, the hands of friends, and for the upbuilding of the village in which they lived. Then work was born of talent and meant for communal generosity. People not only worked together but shared the results of their common endeavors together.

Now, in technological societies, we must look for other ways to develop our talent and at the same time enable others to do something to better their part of this world.

Work is the gift we give to the world. That's why it's so important that what we do for a living has value, not simply for ourselves but for the world at large.

Good work is work that develops us as we develop it. To know if the work we are doing is worth it, we need to ask ourselves what it's bringing out in us: creativity, commitment, artistry, compassion?

The work we do in life is what we leave behind for others to remember us by. It is our legacy to the future. If our work has been good work, it becomes one more brick meant to leave a better tomorrow to those who will come after us.

The fact is that our work shapes us as much as we shape our work. Because of what we do and the way we do it, we become different people than we would have been without it. To know if the work we're doing is leading us to the fullness of ourselves, it's important to ask what we feel we'd lose—other than simply our wages—if we lost that work.

In this society we train young people to look for jobs that make the most money. The problem is that good money is not always the sign of a good job—either for us or for the world around us. Cicero wrote, "If you pursue good with labor, the labor passes away but the good remains; if you pursue evil with pleasure, the pleasure passes away and the evil remains."

Whatever we do—however mundane, however routine, however ephemeral—has dignity and value if we do it as best as it can possibly be done. Cleaning a room, programming the computer and completing a high-level political project are all to be evaluated by the same norms. Was it done honestly? Was it done for the sake of the common good? Was it done well?

Most of us have one gift that shines far and above all our other talents.

Most of us have one gift that shines far and above all our other talents. Sometimes it's technical; sometimes it's physical; sometimes it's social. But whichever it is, that's the work we should be doing. Not any of them should be chosen simply for money.

To steer a child to take a job for profit rather than to enable the blossoming of the soul is to do a disservice to that life. As Elbert Hubbard says, "We work to become, not to acquire."

Good work, the kind of work that makes us happy, is not work that we're paid to do. It's work that we would pay to be allowed to do.

Talent is one thing but excellence is another. It can take a lifetime to make the perfect meringue. It can take a lifetime to shape the perfect pot. It can take a lifetime to find the missing idea—the one that improves on the one we have. But when that day comes, one thing we know for sure: we have not lived in vain. Life is a practiced art. As Samuel Johnson wrote, "Excellence, in any department, can only be attained by the labor of a lifetime. It is not purchased for a lesser price."

Discovering what we are meant to do in the world is our first gift to humankind.

Discovering what we are meant to do in the world is our first gift to humankind. It may take a while to find our real gift and its real purpose, but the excursion is worth the time—for all our sakes. Thomas Carlyle wrote, "The work an unknown good person has done is like a vein of water flowing hidden underground, secretly making the ground green."

The Torah required the Chosen People to deliberately leave food in the field for the sake of those who without it would not have enough to sustain themselves, their families, an honest life. Clearly, at least some part of what we ourselves earn is meant to be given for the welfare of the rest of the community. Without that, the quality of our own lives and our own community is in danger.

When we begin to consider work an unnecessary evil rather than a necessary blessing, we not only lose a sense of our interdependence with the rest of humankind; we lose a sense of the real importance of our own lives.

We don't work to put in time; we don't work to store up wealth; we work to make the world a better place because we ourselves have been here. It's knowing the reason we work that changes the character of the work we do. It becomes a standard for choice. It becomes a mark of our own quality. As Diane Ravitch says, "The person who knows how will always have a job. But the person who knows why will always be the boss."

Vision is the ability to set our course in life. Work is the vehicle that is meant to take us there. One without the other is useless. As Emerson says, "The prize will not be sent to you. You have to win it."

The economic value of work lies only in what we do with the money we get from it. If all we do is spend it on ourselves, that is a very puny life indeed.

There are two things in life that fulfill us. They are not unrelated. Doing what we were born to do and doing what we love to do for the sake of the rest of the world are of a piece. As Theodor Reik says, "Work and love—these are the basics. Without them there is neurosis," a psychological wound to the soul that leaves us depressed about the present and anxious about the future.

Work gives flesh to our dreams and substance to our hopes in life. It makes our goals real and takes us beyond our disappointments.

Work is the blessing we are given in order to be a blessing to others.

Millet's The Gleaners was rejected by his society because it showed the underside of the industrial revolution. It unmasked the dirty little secret that poverty in an industrial society was not an individual problem but a corporate problem, a national problem, an institutional problem. Where some have jobs and many have none, when most eat well but many are forced to glean the nation's garbage cans, the nation is suffering from a disease of the soul that is not only pernicious but may also be terminal, not only for the jobless but for the comfortable complacent as well. What we allow to happen to the least of us will eventually pollute our own lives as well.

Work is a blessing in itself. As Voltaire wrote, "Work keeps at bay three great evils: boredom, vice, and need."

One of the blessings of work is the ability it gives us to give alms, to give dignity to those who, however hard they work, cannot sustain themselves. To deny alms to a person in need is to deny them life. To judge harshly those who cannot provide fully for themselves is to expose our own lack of experience. The God who gives us life without merit expects us to do the same for others. As Emerson noted, "Noblesse oblige; or, superior advantages bind you to larger generosity." At the end of the day, the poor have the responsibility to be responsible, but we have a responsibility that is just as binding. Our responsibility is to be compassionate.

To deny alms to a person in need is to deny them life.

The Haitian proverb teaches, "Rocks in the water don't know the misery of rocks in the sun." To be comfortable ourselves is to risk the life-stopping sin of becoming insensitive to the life-searing distress of others.

Wealth has become a synonym for success in this world. But few ask where the money came from or how it was earned or what is being done with it or how it is affecting the world. And, in the end, that may destroy us all.

"What you do for the least of these, you do for me."

It is not enough simply to sustain people; it is necessary to see them as people and to treat them as people. Otherwise we make commodities of the poor. The Chinese philosopher Mencius wrote: "To feed people and not to love them is to treat them as if they were barnyard cattle. To love them and not to respect them is to treat them as if they were household pets."

"What you do for the least of these, you do for me," Jesus said. The question is how to translate that into political science in this day and age. But one thing is clear. As John F. Kennedy wrote, "If a free society cannot help the many who are poor, it cannot save the few who are rich." Point: Whether we want to admit it or not, we are all in this boat together. And it is sinking.

To balance the national budget on the backs of women and children is a national disgrace, a national sin, and a national mistake of historic proportions. No nation can succeed when its mothers and its children are not equal to its future.

No amount of tax breaks, no amount of industry, no amount of national wealth in the face of national poverty can save the nation. "Teach this triple truth to all: A generous heart, kind speech, and a life of service and compassion," the Buddha teaches, "are the things which renew humanity."

In the face of great national greed, corporate corruption, and the rising levels of working-class poverty, Mother Jones, the Irish woman who helped found one of America's first labor unions, reported the following conversation: "I asked a man in prison once how he happened to be there and he said he had stolen a pair of shoes. I told him that if he had stolen our railroad instead, he would be a United States senator." If only that were funny.

ABOUT THE ARTIST

Jean-François Millet (1814–1875) was a French painter and one of the founders of the Barbizon school in rural France. A child of poor peasants, he grew up working on a farm. Millet is noted for his rural scenes and dignified peasants engaged in labor; he can be categorized as part of the naturalism and realism movements.

OCTOBER

ST. JEROME IN HIS STUDY » BY DOMENICO GHIRLANDAIO » FLORENCE, CHURCH OGNISSANTI

LOVE TO WONDER

Ghirlandaio's St. Jerome in His Study is an oddly provocative piece. At first glance, the work seems to be celebrating mental acuity, intense thought, personal brilliance, the immersion in ideas. And Jerome surely possessed all of these. But he was, too, a great deal more than that.

So then, it dawns: The picture is really about a great deal more than knowledge. It's about the need for finding meaning in the centrifuge of facts in which we live. The more knowledge we have, the more the soul must grapple with the question of what it all means. We have to ask ourselves how much of what we know is essential, is helpful to the human race, is the path to the happier life. We have to ask ourselves how we'll live as a result of what we know. The question "Yes, but what does all this mean to me and thee?" has haunted me since grade school.

Jerome, one of the greatest minds of the fifth-century church, has more the look of awe and mystery in his eyes than he has the look of arrogant certainty. His is a soul overwhelmed by the implications of it all. His is the eye of human limitation in the face of cosmic wonder.

The problem with our time, perhaps, is that we have been seduced by facts and data and, at the same time, become bereft of wonder. We want to know it all rather than to understand the meaning of it all for the good life here and now.

The universe, however technological it may now be, is still the ultimate mystery, the essential human question, the greatest spiritual revelation. Everything else is distraction. To know all the elements, all the chemistry of life, is one thing; to know what it means to live a good life in the midst of the knowledge of what humans can do with these elements to destroy life is entirely another.

Immersion in God requires awe of the limitless, care for the particular, faith in the darkness that is light. And yet we insist on obsessing over the minuscule, the petty, the silly, the neurotic, the useless. God save us.

We need to learn to live with the eye of the brain on the probable and with the other eye, the eye of the soul, on the wonderful mystery that is the gift of life.

We may spend our lives poring over minutiae but underneath it all, we are plagued by the great questions of life, not the small ones. Who am I? Where did I come from? Why am I here? Where am I going? If anywhere at all.

OCTOBER

Without a sense of wonder, we may be living but we are not yet completely alive.

It isn't answers that make life worth living; it is being able to come to a place of spiritual surrender however difficult the questions we face.

To be in awe of something is a very special state of mind. It teaches us our place in the universe and leaves us more able to honor the place of others, as well. It teaches us that life is really about bigger things than ourselves.

The mysteries of life are not meant to defeat us. They are meant to show us that however dull or dry or difficult life may seem to us at any moment, there is always something beyond it that is more

than worth the price of admission. As Thomas Carlyle puts it, "This world, after all our science and sciences, is still a miracle; wonderful, inscrutable, magical and more...."

It is wonder that leads to knowledge, that drives us to discover, that enables us to decipher the world around us. Knowledge is about what is; wonder is about what may be.

If we knew everything about everything, there would be no reason to be alive.

Don't be discouraged by what you don't know. In fact, what we don't know may be one of the only things we really know that is any impetus to tomorrow. "To be conscious that you are ignorant," Benjamin Disraeli said, "is a great step to knowledge."

What we call "knowledge" today is the measure only of what we know now. It is the wisdom to realize that there is always more to learn that makes the human being a growing, living thing. And just as important, perhaps, someone decent to live with!

The value of knowledge is that it is designed to stretch us beyond ourselves and make us productive members of the human community. To eschew knowledge, to refuse to learn, is to be willing to become a parasite on the human race.

The sign of real freedom is the willingness of an institution to put no restrictions or limits on learning. "If we value the pursuit of knowledge," Adlai E. Stevenson wrote, "we must be free to follow wherever that search may lead us. The free mind is not a barking dog, to be tethered on a ten-foot chain."

Beware the society that tells you not to learn, not to question, not to grow beyond the limits of the present, not to think. That is a society that uses one part of itself for the benefit of another part of itself. That's called slavery, no matter who does it.

"If you have knowledge, let others light their candles at it."

The purpose of knowledge is to make the whole world a better place. "If you have knowledge," Margaret Fuller writes, "let others light their candles at it."

"What will learning geometry have to do with the rest of my life?" the student asked. "Not a thing," the teacher said. "But one thing it will do is to develop a particular part of your brain so that in whatever circumstances you find yourself in life, you will have a wholly developed brain with which to figure it out."

Facts have little or nothing to do with real knowledge of a thing.

When we give ourselves over to Mystery—to what we do clearly see but do not understand—we open ourselves to the notion that possibility—what can be—is more important than certainty about what is.

One question leads to another; one fact leads to another; one doubt leads to faith in something else. It is what we do not know that enables us, if we will, to discover the rest of life.

"I'm not interested in learning" is one of the most dangerous remarks in life. It encloses us within ourselves. It drains us of our potential. It leaves us to the mercy of the knowledge of others.

Facts have little or nothing to do with real knowledge of a thing. Facts only tell us what. Knowledge tells us why and so what. Richard Feynman says it all when he says, "You can know the name of a bird in all the languages of the world, but when you're finished, you'll know absolutely nothing whatever about the bird....I learned very early the

difference between knowing the name of something and knowing something."

Taking an inventory of three things we do not
know—like where the stars come from, or how
drugs work on the brain, or how whales navigate
the seas—is one thing. But knowing the implications of those things for our own life is even more.
What if there weren't stars? What if there weren't
drugs? What if whales couldn't navigate? Then,
what would our own lives be like? Those questions
are the difference between fact and wonder.

Learning something leaves us different than we
were before we knew it. Learning is our lifeline to
the fullness of ourselves. "We wake, if ever at all,"
Annie Dillard writes, "to mystery."

To pursue an interest in anything that is independent of our daily lives, our commercial lives,
our professional lives takes us into learning for
its own sake. Most of all, it opens us to the world
of wonders around us, like a child waking up to
being alive. "Those who can no longer pause to
wonder and stand rapt in awe," Einstein says, "are
as good as dead; their eyes are closed."

To learn more about life is to learn more about God.

If the great Mystery of Life is God, then the more we learn about its little mysteries, the more we know about the God-life itself.

Wonder is God's way of getting our attention.

Wonder is not the beginning of doubt. Wonder is the beginning of understanding the things that are really important in life.

We take life for granted. We take the moon for granted. We take rain for granted. We take ourselves for granted. And so we miss the greatest spiritual experience the world has to offer. While we run around doing spiritual things, we miss the spiritual life we're living. The poet Elizabeth Barrett Browning writes: "Earth's crammed with heaven, / And every common bush afire with God: / But only he who sees, takes off his shoes; / The rest sit round it, and pluck blackberries."

Learning to rest in the cosmic reality that the unknown is as important a gift to our development as the known—this is the beginning of the real understanding of life.

It isn't so much collecting the beautiful that counts as it is learning to ponder it. Pondering is the point at which we begin to live at the level of the soul rather than at the level of the appetite alone.

Don't be afraid of what you don't know.

Revel in your questions. Trust them. Follow them. Questions, however heretical they may seem, lead in the end always and only to God.

Don't be afraid of what you don't know. Take it as a sign from God that God is still the one Mystery we are required to trust.

Learning to ask the right questions in life can be a great deal more important to the country, to the planet, to the church than simply repeating yesterday's right answers. As Annie Dillard puts it, "We have been as usual asking the wrong question. It does not matter a hoot what the mockingbird on the chimney is singing. The real and proper question is: Why is it beautiful?"

*Be care-
ful lest
knowledge
delude you
into think-
ing that
you know
something.*

Be careful lest knowledge delude you into thinking that you know something. As the proverb
says,

*He who knows not, and knows not that
    he knows not,
        is a fool. Shun him.*
*She who knows not, and knows that she knows not,
        is simple. Teach her.*
*He who knows, and knows not that he knows,
        is asleep. Wake him.*
*She who knows, and knows that she knows,
        is wise. Follow her.*

NOVEMBER

IN THE RAIN » BY FRANZ MARC » MÜNCHEN, STÄDTISCHE GALERIE

TO LOOK AT
A THING

Soul blindness is a terminal disease. The person who is soul-blind sees everything and everyone around them as if they were cardboard cutouts, one-dimensional, without sides or depth or shades of grey.

But it is those who know that what we can see with our eyes is only one facet of life, who stretch and bend and color life for the rest of us. They know that there is more than one way to make a thing real. There is more than any one single insight into one single facet of life.

The gift of seeing differently is a very special gift in life, one to be cultivated, one to be sought after, one to be celebrated.

Artists have for years shown us how to see differently, how to think differently, how to construct our worlds differently. Early 20th-century German Expressionist Franz Marc's *In the Rain* uses wild color, fluid lines, vibrant diagonals, and a swirling collection of vegetation, animals, and human profiles to capture the fury of nature, as well as the psalmist's cry that the rain falls on good and bad alike. It enables us to feel the rain, to know the storm, to realize our identity with nature.

To be able to look at something and imagine how to do it differently is the gift that frees the soul. No, it's more than that.We come to understand there is no one way, no right way to do something, to understand something, to think about something, to reimagine something. There are as many ways as there are people. In fact, we all see everything differently. The challenge is to free imagination in ourselves. Then we, too, can begin to see the "perhaps" in a thing, a person, an institution, a plan, as well as its ghost from the past.

We live in a century that bursts with creativity: First we put computers in machines the size of a room, then into machines the size of a closet, then into machines the size of a suitcase, and now into machines the size of a pinhead. And all of those changes came within 50 years.

Each of them in less than any single lifetime. All of them before we got accustomed to the one before it.

To have a world such as this is to have a living icon of the possible.

So why, I need to ask myself, do we keep trying to reinvent the past, to deny that it has changed, to forget that change is organic? That each new thing comes out of what came before it.

Beware any institution that teaches that yesterday is forever. That yesterday is better than tomorrow. That yesterday is holier, better, purer, more the voice of God than now. That to think about something differently is to deny the God who made creativity and growth and change a necessary part of life.

But first, it is a matter of beginning to see what is underneath, what is more than what we see on the surface of life. That's creativity.

NOVEMBER

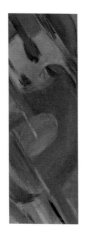

What a thing appears to be is nice; what it might become if I allowed it the freedom to grow in a different direction is nothing less than a miracle.

We are told that someone asked Michelangelo how he could sculpt such beautiful statues and he said, "I saw the angel in the marble and carved until I set him free." How's that for all the people who want us to see only the marble in the marble?

Creativity is the burst of the creator in the creature that makes the world new again—for all our sakes.

The ability to see life, problems, people newly, to see the possibilities in them rather than the problems, makes life an eternal adventure. It is the investment of life in one unending list of daily experiments in hope.

Everyone has the ability to be creative. All we need to do is to learn to play with shapes and colors and ideas. It's what first grade is all about. Until we learn the rules, of course.

Everyone has the ability to be creative.

When what has always been becomes more important than what might be, institutions die, relationships die, excitement dies.

There are architects now who are building buildings that don't look like buildings anymore—a see-through house, a floating opera house in Sydney Harbor, an apartment building whose floors are of uneven height. Why? So we can all learn to live outside the boxes into which our minds have been cemented.

When someone says, "Well, you certainly can't do that!" there is only one possible intelligent response: "Why not?" Then we all can begin to think again. As Doctor Seuss says, "Fantasy is a

necessary ingredient in living. It's a way of looking at life through the wrong end of a telescope.
Which is what I do, and that enables you to laugh
at life's realities." Theodor Geisel (Dr. Seuss)

When what was becomes more important than
what is, we doom ourselves to a life full of perpet-
ual yesterdays. And the dull, slow, robotized mind
that goes with them.

Yesterday is fine for yesterday. But what does it have to do with today?

Yesterday is fine for yesterday. But what does it
have to do with today? Unless we are sure we
know the answer and are committed to doing
it, it's time to start thinking of new ways to do
old things so that the real value of the old can be
maintained.

Sometimes it is necessary to change in order to go
on being who we are.

When we release within ourselves the ability to
re-imagine our own lives—life without this house,
this job, this place, this way of going through the
day—we begin the slow, simmering process of
real thinking. Then whatever we decide to do can
become of our own making rather than shackles
of someone else's design.

Daydreaming is the fine art of rethinking and recreating life. As Edgar Allen Poe wrote, "Those who dream by day are cognizant of many things which escape those who dream only by night."

When we start our lives with "no" or "can't" or "impossible," we make life more a ghost than a spirit. We pretend to be alive but we have actually succumbed to slow death. As Jean-Luc Picard says, "Things are only impossible until they're not."

Just because an idea is new does not make it good. But it doesn't make it bad either. The trick lies in allowing an idea enough time to prove itself. It's what Jesus means when he says, "By their fruits you shall know them."

Refusing to give up an idea—any idea—without testing or trying it is the sign of a mind in which rigor mortis has set in. The only problem with that is that we just might be killing other people along with it by denying them a chance for a better, happier life.

Creativity is not about revolution; it is about evolution. About taking an old idea and making it better for its times. "Discovery," Albert Szent-

Györgyi wrote, "consists of seeing what everybody has seen and thinking what nobody has thought."

Don't be afraid to think differently from the people around you. Be afraid of what will be lost because you were afraid to think, and rethink, and think again of ways to make what is now necessary, real.

When we take the tried-and-true for granted—as if in it all possibilities have been exhausted—we destroy life that is trying to be born. We cut off tomorrow without ever even giving it a try.

The poet e.e. cummings teaches, "All creation begins with destruction." The point is that we must be willing to let the past go for awhile in order to try out another way of being alive.

If the world is going to get better because we've been here, it only stands to reason that we each need to do something to make it so: clean up the streets, mow the lawn, think of a better way to recycle the garbage, grow an organic tomato, plant a tree, figure out a better way to teach a child math and get groceries to shut-ins, perhaps.

Learn to look at something—at anything—and wonder what the rest of your life would be like if it were round instead of square, blue instead of colorless, now instead of later, gone instead of here. Then figure out what you would need to do to adjust to that. Would life be better? Worse? About the same?

Fear is the great impediment to life. "I dreamed a thousand new paths," the Chinese say. "I woke and walked my old one." The question is, Why?

"Because we've always done it that way" is the death knell of life. Avoid it like the plague.

Fear is the great impediment to life.

What we think might work, or ought to work, or should work, may very well work. Whether anyone else but you thinks so or not. Try it, why don't you? As Aristotle said, "Intuition is the source of scientific knowledge." Not the other way around.

It isn't how many times we fail when we try something new that counts. It's the one time that succeeds that makes all the difference. As John Dewey said, "Every great advance in science has issued from a new audacity of imagination."

It's daring to think about other ways to do things; that is the well of creativity.

"It is the creative potential itself in human beings that is the image of God," Mary Daly writes. But if we really believed that, we would stop trying to stamp it out in the people around us. We would know that there were multiple ways to express the same thing—by color for rain, like Marc's painting, perhaps—or music for pain, maybe—or curved lines instead of square ones for a building. We would cultivate the gift of learning to see the world in new ways.

We begin, as children, by creating a world full of other worlds in our heads.

We begin, as children, by creating a world full of other worlds in our heads. Then someone feels obliged to tell us that we're not allowed to do that anymore. And our once colorful and fanciful life goes to black and white. Then we have to learn to think "right"—translate "dull," "routine," "rigid."

Someday, look at some object in front of you and imagine another way of building, painting, describing it. Lewis Carroll, famed author of Alice in Wonderland put it this way:

"When you are describing,
  A shape, or sound, or tint;

Don't state the matter plainly,
  But put it in a hint;
And learn to look at all things,
  With a sort of mental squint."

Get it? That's creativity.

ABOUT THE ARTIST

Franz Marc (February 8, 1880–March 4, 1916) was a German painter and printmaker, one of the key figures of the German Expressionist movement. Most of his mature work portrays animals, usually in natural settings. His work is characterized by bright primary color, an almost cubist portrayal of animals, stark simplicity and a profound sense of emotion. He was killed in World War I at the age of 36.

ADORATION OF THE SHEPHERDS » BY FGERRIT VAN HONTHORST » KÖLN, WALLRAF-RICHARTZ-MUSEUM

O Come Let
Us Adore...

"All rulers will pay homage,
And all nations will serve your anointed."

PSALM 72:11

What we adore in life is what determines the quality of our lives. To adore money is to live in unremitting, unsatisfied greed. To adore sex is to live in restless lust devoid of love, centered in the pleasures of the self. To adore power is to live in fear of the loss of it and out of touch with the gifts of those around us. Those things become more and more obvious as life goes by.

But it was as I sat and rested in Honthorst's *Adoration of the Shepherds* that I realized that even religion can make itself a replacement for life in God. In fact, a kind of pseudo-holiness can be a very clever substitution of the self for the real goal of life. We can stop far short of holiness in a self-satisfying morass of false piety.

Notice, for instance, who is in the picture. Better yet, notice who is not in the picture. There are no potentates here, none of the privileged, no social elites, not even any great religious figures from the Temple. Just shepherds.

What's wrong with this picture? What's wrong is that shepherds are one of the lowest ranks of early society. Unlike land-owning farmers, shepherds were wage-earning nomads, hired hands, nobodies. It is these who were attached to nothing in either town or temple who could recognize goodness when they saw it in the most unusual of places in the most unusual of people while thousands adored at other shrines in life and did not.

I understand the power of the picture. I adore the fearless, kind, embracing, challenging Jesus. Therefore, I am not fit for anything, not even a church, that purports to be a surrogate for the center of life. Any church that wants us to bow down and say, "You, the Church, are God" asks us to adore something less than God.

With the shepherds who were the first to see Jesus, to hear in their hearts the anthem of his arrival, I can only say in my heart that God is God. And even more: though Jesus may be male, God who is "pure spirit," they tell us, is not. Not even in a church that makes God so.

No doubt about it: What we adore in life determines who we are and what we become in the life-long search for the God who is searching for us. To be the fullness of what God means for us to be, we must beware of letting anything less dim that in us.

DECEMBER

False idols are everywhere these days: in newspapers, on TV ads, on billboards, in magazines, in the margins of every website, even on the phone. They are meant to excite us and arrest us and, they hope, seduce us. It's not what we pass up because we can't afford it that counts. It's what we pass up because we don't need it even when we can afford it. Then we know we are free.

It's important to be aware of what consumes us in life. That's the only way we have a clue about what we might be missing. Then we get to make some choices to do other things.

To be alive means to be alert to everything around us: not dull to some, dead to others, uncaring of the rest. Life has to do with doing more of what gives a sense of new energy to every part of us. It also means, then, that we must learn to do less of what does not—to what only robotizes our bodies or deadens our minds and souls.

To worship at the shrine of an addiction, any addiction, is to give ourselves over to what we think we control but which will eventually control us instead.

Addictions seduce because at first it seems that they sweeten what is already dead in us. Wild shopping or heavy drinking or soothing drugs take away the pain of what we refuse to address otherwise. It's when we start coming down the other side of them that the pain sets in and we find ourselves in chains.

To be in thrall to anything is to miss the rest of everything in life. "The truly important things in life—love, beauty, and one's own uniqueness—are constantly," Pablo Casals says, "being overlooked." But what we overlook is always what we're missing in life.

Too much openness is every bit as bad as too much rigidity in life. It's learning to say both yes and no to everything that is the real secret to the good life. "The trick is in what one emphasizes," Carlos Castaneda says. "We either make ourselves miserable or we make ourselves happy. The amount of work is the same."

"We either make ourselves miserable or we make ourselves happy. The amount of work is the same."

Christmas is about making happiness—making whatever we have all we want, all we need—rather than making accumulation the center of life.

When we discover the other part of life—the spiritual part of life—all the false shrines we've built lose their luster. Then our eyes are opened and we begin to see everything we do have rather than everything we don't.

God is everywhere but it is the shepherds of life—
the simple ones, the steady ones, the ones who
live closest to earth and move closer to heaven
at the same time—who can tell what is real from
what is bogus. It is these types who love the world
of things but never fail to develop the world of the
spirit at the same time.

*The love of
life leads
to a love
of worship,
of relation-
ship with
the Giver
of the Gift
of Life.*

It's important to love something in life; it is
equally important not to try to capture it. Let life
fly from tree to tree along the way.

The love of life leads to a love of worship, of
relationship with the Giver of the Gift of Life. "It
is in the process of being worshipped," C.S. Lewis
writes, "that God communicates the divine presence to humanity."

We become what we adore: sodden with indul-
gence or bursting with life. "Worship," Jack Hayford
writes, "changes the worshipper into the image of
the One worshipped." That's why it is so important
to decide where, to what, and to whom we build
our idols.

As we go from one altar of worship to another we
are really only looking for God. It is what we make

our gods out of, however, that determines the kind of person we ourselves will be. The mystic Julian of Norwich says of the process: "Until I am essentially united with God, I can never have full rest or real happiness."

Agitation, the constant need for more and other and still more, is a signal of the restless heart, the soul without boundaries, the spirit without a center. "Home," Emily Dickinson says, "is the definition of God." Then, when, like the shepherds, we attach ourselves to the purpose of life, rather than its superfluities, we know that the journey has been worth it...and peace comes.

What surprised the shepherds was not that the Messiah would come or the angels had called them or the divine presence was in a baby. What surprised them was that God had come to the very place where they had always been. The process is the same for us. Wherever we go to find Life, the fact is that Life is already within us if we will only attend to it.

It is coming to see the wonders around us that leads to a wonder-full life. As the Sufi poet Hafiz says of it: "Slipping on my shoes, boiling water, toasting bread, buttering the sky: That should

be enough contact with God in one day to make anyone crazy."

Don't be disturbed because you can't explain God, or see God, or understand God, or capture God on the end of a star. The very fact you realize there is a mystery is itself enough of an answer to the universe.

The awareness that there is more, that there must be more, is the proof of God planted in our hearts. It is the search for that God who is already with us that leads us to worship at altars made of clay along the way.

It is doubt itself that is the foundation of faith. "At the moment you are most in awe of all there is about life that you don't understand," Jane Wagner writes, "you are closer to understanding it all than at any other time." When we are finally no longer sure of all the answers, we are open to recognizing the final one.

The Mystery we call God is all around us. Everywhere. The great lesson of the spiritual life is to learn to drink it in, in all its colors, all its shapes, all its tastes. "O taste and see that the Lord is good," the Scriptures teach. It's just a matter of learning to love each of the many ways of tasting the God in whose mystery we dwell. "One cannot speak about mystery," René Magritte writes. "One must be seized by it."

We spend so much time in life struggling to find a secret key by which to experience God, when all we need is to appreciate the God who dwells in us and with us where we are. Richard Kehl tells a story about the Buddha: Siddhartha Gautama once cried out in pity for a yogi by the river who had wasted twenty years of his human existence in learning how to walk on water, when the ferryman might have taken him across for a small coin. Point: God is all around us—just waiting for us to notice.

To call God a Mystery does not mean that God does not exist.

To call God a Mystery does not mean that God does not exist. It simply means that God is greater than anything we can possibly understand. It is the very act of unknowing that takes us into the Great Unknown.

Where is God? There. No, here. All at once particular and universal, seen and unseen, present and absent. As Lorenz Oken puts it: "The universe is the language of God."

If God is all Being, then we are swimming, all together and at once, in the very womb of God. What can possibly be more real, more exciting? Only then can we be caught up, wide-eyed, like shepherds in front of a baby, with the awesome thunderous awareness of the invisible God.

Instead of giving our lives over to life, we give them away to things that do not matter.

It is so easy to get immersed in what is outside of us that we ignore entirely what is inside of us, calling us, prodding us on, companioning us as we go.

God is not "out there" anymore than God is "in here." God is beyond place and by that very fact is everywhere. It is not God who does not come to us. We are the ones who are missing in action.

Instead of giving our lives over to life, we give them away to things that do not matter, do not last, are at best passing, reduce us to living in chains we make for ourselves: clothes, jewelry, money, status, power, drugs, alcohol—all of them good and all of them temporary and all of them dangerous if taken to extremes.

124

In Gerrit van Honthorst's Adoration of the
Shepherds we see what it is to be captivated by
the magnet that is God. Then the kind of life that
enjoys life begins.

When we get to the point in life that we realize
that things have almost nothing to do with happiness, joy takes over and peace comes to stay.
Thomas Merton says, "Life is this simple: we are
living in a world that is absolutely transparent
and God is shining through it all the time....If
we abandon ourselves to God and forget ourselves, we see it sometimes, and we see it maybe
frequently."

Christmas isn't a holiday. Christmas is a way of
being alive. "Christmas is not a time nor a season,"
Calvin Coolidge said. "It is a state of mind. To cher-
ish peace and goodwill, to be plenteous in mercy
is to have the real spirit of Christmas." Merry
Christmas to you all—every day of the year.

Gerrit van Honthorst (1592–1656), also known as Gerard van Honthorst, was a popular and prolific Dutch Golden Age painter from Utrecht. His most attractive pieces are those in which he cultivates the style of the Italian artist Caravaggio, often painting scenes illuminated by a single candle.

ALSO BY JOAN CHITTISTER

ASPECTS OF THE HEART *The Many Paths to a Good Life*
In this lovely book, Sr. Joan looks at 50 "aspects" all of which in some way can fill our hearts and our lives. She talks about a prayerful heart, a peaceful heart, a risking heart, a wise heart, a cosmic heart, a compassionate heart. Each brief chapter offers abundant food for reflection and prayer, and each offers an opportunity to become persons who "produce Good from the treasure of the heart" (Luke 6:45).
HARDCOVER | 112 PAGES | $12.95 | 978-1-58595-871-9

....

SONGS OF THE HEART *Reflections on the Psalms*
Sister Joan offers poignant, challenging reflections on 25 psalms, each offering a spiritual oasis away from the stresses of the world. In praying and reflecting on these psalms, readers will find new meaning at the core of life. Great spiritual reading for all who long to pray the psalms more deeply and attentively.
HARDCOVER | 136 PAGES | $12.95 | 978-1-58595-835-1

....

GOD'S TENDER MERCY *Reflections on Forgiveness*
Here Sister Joan tackles the virtue of mercy and its vital connection to forgiveness. She invites readers to stop judging, accusing, and criticizing "sinners," and to see themselves in their number. This challenging and inspiring book is spiritual reading at its very best.
HARDCOVER | 80 PAGES | $10.95 | 978-1-58595-799-6

....

THE BREATH OF THE SOUL *Reflections on Prayer*
This simple yet profound book is an examination of what we ourselves must bring to the discipline of prayer—whatever form it takes—in order to make prayer a deep and integral part of our lives. Great spiritual reading for all who long for prayer to be at the core of their lives.
HARDCOVER | 144 PAGES | $12.95 | 978-1-58595-747-7

1-800-321-0411
www.23rdpublications.com